Filling a Little Space

The Susanna Wesley Story

Chrystal Stauffer

Illustrated by Olivia and Bethany Moy

Helping Children See Jesus

biblevisuals.org

Our mission: To produce and provide visualized curriculum to ministry partners worldwide

Bible Visuals International exists to produce curriculum that is gospel-focused, scripturally sound and visually excellent and to provide it to our ministry partners worldwide in ways that are affordable, accessible and adaptable to their needs.

Our vision: Helping Children See Jesus

Bible Visuals International envisions that all children would have the opportunity to trust Jesus Christ as their Savior and to experience God's redemptive power in their lives.

BVI is a 501(c)(3) charity organization. We rely on the support of ministry partners like you to help us in our mission. If you would like to learn more, please visit our website at **biblevisuals.org**.

Page layout & design: Aaron Housenga

© 2020 Bible Visuals International
PO Box 153, Akron, PA 17501-0153
717.859.1131

biblevisuals.org

ISBN: 978-1-64104-122-5

All rights reserved. Printed in the United States of America.
International copyright regulations apply. No duplication for resale allowed.
No part of this book may be reproduced without written permission except where indicated.

Filling a Little Space

The Susanna Wesley Story

Filling a Little Space 4
Memory Verse 25
Map 27
Review Questions 28

Filling a Little Space
The Susanna Wesley Story

Susanna rubbed her swollen belly and wondered how much longer it would be before this little one decided to join them. She was seven months pregnant. Glancing around the small kitchen, she noticed that the fire burning in the brick fireplace needed to be stirred, the chairs needed to be straightened and her plant in the corner needed to be watered. Those can wait, she told herself as she thought about how little food they had on hand at the moment and that there would still be hungry little bellies to fill at dinner. She was just thankful they had a roof over their heads. They had been in debt for a long time, and it seemed that no matter what her husband Samuel did, they couldn't get ahead.

In 1697, they had moved to Epworth, Lincolnshire (map page 27) hoping to get a fresh start, but after more than ten years there they were still in debt. There was always another trip Samuel needed to take as the minister, another crop that had failed and yet another mouth to feed.

Susanna didn't mind being poor, but she did hate it when people criticized her husband for not providing well for the family.

Yes, their house was small, their food scarce and their possessions few, but she was content. Her happiness came from knowing God and being known by Him. She prayed that her children would know this same happiness.

This baby she was carrying was number 19 for her and Samuel! Despite the fact she was weary and felt as if she'd been sick and pregnant for most of their married life, she wasn't going to take this little one for granted. Though illness, disease and tragedy were common in those days, nine of her 19 children were already buried, most of them as infants, and Susanna knew that each day with her remaining children was a gift. She breathed a quick prayer. "Thank you, Lord. I know that 'tis no small honor to be entrusted with the care of so many souls."

Follow the QR Code for activities, games, and other resources related to this story!

The kitchen door was suddenly flung open by Susanna's daughter Hetty. The girl paused in the doorway breathless. Susanna was about to scold her for disturbing the peace when she noticed that the girl's eyes were filled with tears. "Why, Hetty, whatever is the matter?" she questioned. "It's Father," Hetty wailed and her body shook with sobs. "Someone just came to say that they've taken him again!" "Who's taken him?" Susanna inquired calmly as she moved to her daughter's side. Hetty flung herself into the arms of her mother. "They've arrested him and said they are taking him to jail again because of his debt," Hetty finally managed to get out.

Susanna took a deep breath and quietly stroked her daughter's hair to calm her. It also gave her time to gather her own thoughts. This wasn't the first time Samuel had been arrested and taken to debtors' prison. Unless someone sent money to pay off the debt, he'd have to stay in the prison until he could work it off there. From around the corner of the hallway, she could see three or four more curious little faces sticking their heads out, watching the scene before them unfold. "Mother, are we really so poor? Can they just take Father away like that?" Hetty asked, lifting her head and sniffing. "Yes, Hetty, we are. And yes, they can." Susanna answered honestly. This brought more tears. "Oh why does this have to happen to us? What are we ever going to do? And Mother, what have we done to deserve this? Why does God allow such things to happen?" Hetty couldn't stop the questions from flowing. Susanna gently held Hetty at arm's length so she could look her in the face. "Listen, Hetty. As long as we have God, it doesn't really matter what's going on or where we are. God is enough. You must trust in His love and goodness. Now, dry your tears. We shall have no more of those. There is nothing we can do for the time being but wait to hear from your father."

Suddenly feeling the strong need to pray, Susanna sent Hetty on her way before throwing her apron over her head and sinking onto a stool. Her children knew that they were not to disturb her whenever the apron was over her head, so she could be guaranteed some quiet for the time being.

Despite what she had said to Hetty, she could feel the discouragement and fear in her own heart. Many years on her knees had brought her to the realization that prayer was her greatest weapon during such battles. As a child, she'd made a commitment that for every hour she spent in entertainment, she would spend one hour with God in prayer and in the Word. Now, as an adult, she found this was impossible. Instead, she'd decided to spend two hours a day in prayer. In her mind, this was time well spent. So often she found herself needing wisdom or peace. *Oh God,* her heart moaned. *I know that You are here. Help me to endure this well. You know how much harder it is for me to feed the family when this happens. Help my children's faith in You to be strengthened through this trial as we see You provide once more. Lord, I am content to fill a little space if You are glorified.*

An hour later, Susanna rose from the stool feeling much refreshed. God was able. He would carry them through. And carry them He did. After a few weeks in prison, Samuel was released due to various people's sending money on his behalf.

However, their troubles were far from over.

One night after everyone had long been asleep, Susanna's eyes flew open, and she bolted upright in the bed. What had awakened her? She could hear Hetty's voice calling out loudly and urgently. She took a brief moment to gather her bearings, then she smelled it. Smoke! Something was burning! She stumbled out of bed, her mind racing as she thought of the children. Samuel had already beaten her to the door.

Throwing it open, they saw thick smoke and flames licking at the roof. "There's no time to gather anything!" Samuel cried urgently. "We must get out now!" Susanna rushed into the hall, calling for their maid, Betty, to gather the children from the nursery. Being eight months pregnant, Susanna knew she would be of little help to the maid and that it was urgent for her to get out of the smoke. Rushing downstairs, Susanna tried to make it out the front door, but the wind was so strong that it blew the flames directly toward her. The heat was so intense! Three times Susanna tried to break through the flames but was driven back. Finally, on the fourth attempt, she gathered her skirts tightly around herself and forged ahead. She could feel the heat scorching her legs and face, but she pushed on. Suddenly she felt the heat subsiding and the cool night air hitting her face. She'd made it!

Susanna gazed wildly about, searching for Samuel and the children. No one! The yard was empty! She hurried around the side of the house, frantically scanning the garden. Relief flooded her heart as she saw several of her children standing a safe distance from the house. "Where's your father?" she asked as she gathered some of her littlest children in her arms. Patty, the second youngest, pointed to the house just as Samuel emerged, coughing and sputtering. "It's no use," he said, gasping for air. "John is still in the nursery. I could hear him crying but there is no way for me to get to him." Susanna felt like her heart was tearing in two as she thought about her little John left in the fire.

By this time several men from the town had gathered to help. Suddenly they heard a voice calling from the upstairs window. Looking up they could see John's little face peering out at them. Somehow he had managed to crawl up and break out the window! One of the men shouted, "Quickly! Let's see if we can make it up to him from the outside." There was no time to fetch a ladder, so one man was hoisted up on the shoulders of another. He pulled John into his arms just as there was a loud splintering sound. Suddenly the roof crashed into the nursery! The place where John had been only seconds before was engulfed in flames!

Susanna sank to the ground as she gathered John into her arms. "Thank you, God!" she cried aloud, as tears streamed down her face. "You've saved him, just like a brand plucked from the fire." She didn't know for what purpose God had allowed John's life to be spared, but in her heart she made a vow to particularly care for his little soul.

Lord, help me to teach him true religion and the way that he should live so that his life can bring You honor. And Lord, please give me the grace I'm going to need to do it carefully and sincerely.

Moments later, the whole Wesley family huddled together, watching their home go up in flames.

In the weeks that followed, work began on a new house. During that

time, Susanna gave birth to their last child, a girl named Kezia. For the time being, the other children were sent to live with family and friends. Susanna dearly missed having her children with her.

Within a year they were able to move into a new home. While it was a much larger and solidly built brick house (see map), the cost of building had only pushed them further into debt. Still, Susanna was just happy to have the whole family back together again. However there was much work to be done. She noticed that while the children had been apart, they had forgotten many of the habits she had worked so hard to establish.

In the past, eating had always been restricted to meal times, friends had always been monitored, her children had always been required to sit still during family worship. Bedtime had always been at 8:00 p.m. sharp. Now the children were used to looser schedules, more freedom and had become silly and rude.

For Susanna, these habits were more than just keeping an orderly home. They were ways to teach the children that life was not about serving themselves and being self-focused. She prayed that submission to these house rules would help lead them to submission to God's authority.

In order to help them with their behavior, Susanna decided to set aside time to individually meet with each child for one hour a week. She wanted to provide opportunities to have spiritual discussions with them without all the other children hearing their private conversation. In the process, she found that she got to know them better as individuals, which was something she treasured. As she began school lessons with her children and they grew accustomed to being at home again, Susanna's heart rejoiced to see them thriving once more.

"Charles! Pay attention!" Susanna's strong voice broke through the quiet afternoon, causing the other children in the classroom to raise their heads from their work. Charles shook his head to clear his mind from daydreaming and forced himself to pay attention to the work at hand. He knew it would do him little good to complain that he was tired of studying or that it was much too warm in the classroom to think. His mother would hear none of it. She worked hard to teach all of her children, and playing during school hours was most certainly not tolerated. Even from the time of his earliest memories, his mother had never given them anything they cried for. She gave them only what she thought was good for them. Even then they were required to ask politely for it. Charles snuck a quick peek out the window to see where the sun was in the sky and estimated it to be about 4:00 in the afternoon. Only one hour left and then he'd be free! He could do this! Diligently, he bent his head over his books.

Susanna smiled quietly to herself as she watched her children at work. Oh, how she loved them! Because of her firmness, she knew they didn't always understand that love. She felt her responsibility as a mother weighing heavily on her. At times she feared she would fail to be as committed as she ought. However, her children knew what to expect from her, and in turn, she made great efforts to praise and reward their good behavior. She was also a firm believer in keeping all promises that she made to her children and this helped them to trust her. Susanna checked the time: 5:00 p.m. on the dot. "All right children, you may put your things away. Let's sing a psalm and read from Isaiah 53. Then we'll be done for today."

As her children's sweet voices filled the room, Susanna saw how earnestly Charles sang. While they were too poor to have any instruments of their own, he had always loved music. She wondered how God was going to use that gift of his in the future.

Many years passed.

One by one Susanna watched her children grow up and leave the home. Following a serious fall from a carriage, Samuel passed away, leaving Susanna penniless and in debt. This forced Susanna out of her home and left her to trust God with her needs. Over the next seven years she went to live with her children, going from one home to the next.

She continued to keep in touch with her children by writing letters that offered advice, spiritual thoughts and love. Even though she gave advice, the older she grew and the more she studied God's Word, Susanna realized how little she actually knew! However, this did not stop her desire to pour her life into her children and to see them follow the ways of God. She knew that this alone would bring them happiness.

Her children wrote back, and by this method they kept in touch. However, while letters kept her informed, Susanna missed seeing their faces. She especially longed to see Charles and John. Both of them had become preachers and were busy traveling, so visits were few and far between. After one such visit with Charles at his home in Bristol (see map), she realized that every time she was around him, she was spiritually encouraged. So while his visits were seldom, she found she could never blame him. She knew that what he was doing was worthwhile and that God was blessing his ministry in ways she could never have imagined. And so it was that even while she missed her boys, she didn't wish for anything to change.

Finally a time came when John was able to take a turn supporting his mother. He'd first established a church in Bristol (see map) but then moved to London where he bought a former cannon factory called The Foundry. He used a large part of it for a meetinghouse where he could hold services. The smaller part he turned into his living quarters. While there, Susanna began attending his services. Since the time that she had been a little girl she had only ever attended the Church of England where the emphasis was strongly on works. As she spent more time with John, Susanna became aware of the change that had come over both Charles and John. They now had confidence and assurance of their salvation which seemed to energize them. They trusted that salvation was a "gift of God, not of works" and that it was for "whosoever believeth."

One Sunday, as she sat in the meeting-house listening to a guest speaker, Susanna heard the phrase "The blood of our Lord Jesus Christ which was given for thee." Suddenly she felt her heart struck by the profound truth that "God for Christ's sake hath forgiven you." Her salvation didn't depend on how good a person she had been. It was the work of Christ on the cross that saved her from eternal separation from God. It was His work and nothing more. She had to confess that sometimes she had acted like her salvation was dependent on her success or failure as a mother.

Bowing her head silently, she let the tears stream down her face. *Oh Lord, I have known You all these years, and yet I have never been hit so deeply by the fact that my salvation has nothing to do with my works. I have tried so hard to live a life that is pleasing to You and to teach my children to do the same. Yet that isn't enough. You are so holy and so perfect that nothing I could ever do would gain me the right to know You. Thank you that in Your perfect plan You sent me a Rescuer, Your Son Jesus Christ Who lived a perfect life in my place. I am accepted because of Him. Oh thank You!*

When Susanna was old and knew that her time on earth was coming to an end, she had one simple request: "Children, as soon as I am released, sing a psalm of praise to God." And that's just what they did. As soon as her spirit left this world, her children gathered around her bed. As they had so often done during their childhood school days, they sang a psalm together, praising and worshipping God.

Many years later, John found himself kneeling in front of his mother's grave (see map), wishing he could talk to his mother just one more time. He wished he could tell her all that had happened to him and how much she had impacted the man he'd become. After John had realized that salvation was not by works, many other people also began to understand this truth. John didn't even realize what was happening when God began to use his incredible organizational skills. The Foundry was soon replaced by an even larger chapel in London (see map), but before he knew it he had become the leader of a worldwide movement known as Methodism. As a result, many people were growing in their understanding of truth.

John didn't know yet that he would preach over 40,000 sermons in his lifetime. He also didn't know that his brother, Charles Wesley, would go on to write 6,000 hymns, many of which we still sing today: "Depth of Mercy," "Jesus, Lover of my Soul" and the most popular one, "Hark! The Herald Angels Sing."

What John did know for sure was that he had been greatly affected by his mother's example.

As he read the words on her tombstone written by his brother, John nodded his head in silent agreement:

In sure and steadfast hope to rise,
And claim her mansion in the skies,
A Christian here her flesh laid down,
The cross exchanging for a crown.

Susanna had endured many trials in her life and had very few possessions at her death, but now? Now, she was enjoying a heavenly home that could never be taken away.

In the little space of her home and her life Susanna had filled her children's lives with a godly influence. It was seen in her dependence upon God in those hard times. It was seen in the time, structure and advice she gave her children. It was seen in her own tender heart as God continued to teach her and help her grow in her own faith. As John stood there, he remembered what his mother had often said: "I am content to fill a little space if God be glorified."

John laid his hand on the stone and whispered,

"To God be the glory."

And whatsoever ye do in word or deed, do all in the name of the Lord Jesus, giving thanks to God and the Father by Him.

Colossians 3:17

Map Notes

All of the images on the map are mentioned in the text, and are all related historical sites that still exist today.

- The Old Rectory–This is the house built for the Wesley family following the fire in the story. It was much larger and solidly built than the house destroyed in the fire. However, the expenses incurred in building it put the Wesley family farther in debt.
- The New Room Chapel–This is the oldest Methodist building in the world. John Wesley established a meeting house in Bristol in 1739, but the church soon outgrew it. The New Room Chapel was built in 1748 and is still used for regular service. It houses a museum as well.
- Charles Wesley's Home–Close to the New Room Chapel is the No. 4 Charles Street house, the home that Charles and Sally Wesley lived in with their family. It also houses a museum focused on the family and the history of hymn writing.
- John Wesley's Chapel–As mentioned in the story, the Wesley's first church in London was established at The Foundry, a former brass cannon casting site. In 1778 this new chapel was built nearby.
- Susanna Wesley's Grave–This is located in Bunhill Fields near the Wesley Chapel in London. Bunhill Fields is also the grave site of John Bunyan and Isaac Watts. The headstone pictured in the story was later replaced by a new headstone with a different inscription.

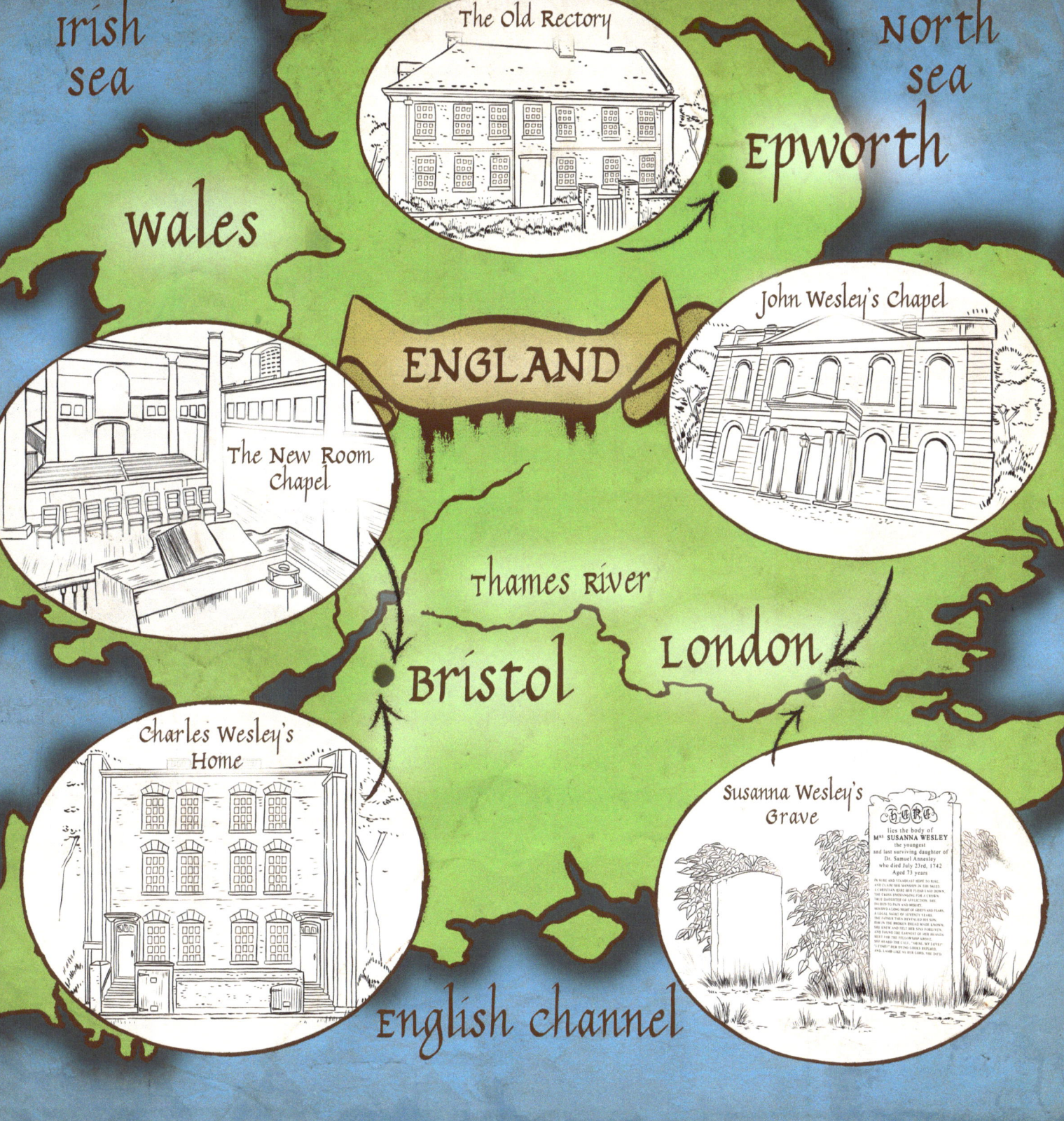

Review Questions

1. In the beginning of the story, what was Susanna Wesley most worried about as she waited for her new baby to be born? *(Her family was very poor, and they had borrowed a lot of money.)*

2. How many children did Susanna and her husband Samuel have? *(She was pregnant with her 19th child, but nine of them had already died.)*

3. What bad news did Susanna's daughter Hetty tell her about her husband Samuel? *(He had been arrested and put in jail because he could not pay back the money he had borrowed.)*

4. Whenever Susanna put her apron over her head, her children knew not to interrupt her. What was she doing? *(Praying; she spent hours talking to God.)*

5. What terrible thing caused Susanna and Samuel to wake up in the middle of the night? *(Their house was on fire.)*

6. How was Susanna's son John rescued from the upstairs nursery? *(A man was hoisted up to the window and John was pulled out.)*

7. What did Susanna do after they were all together again in their new home to make sure she had time with each one of her children? *(She talked with them alone for one hour every week.)*

8. Who was the teacher for the Wesley children, and where did they go to school? *(Their mother, Susanna, taught them at home.)*

9. What was something that Susanna and her children did at the end of their school day that her son Charles especially loved? *(They sang a song of praise to God.)*

10. When Susanna's children grew up, her husband died and she was very poor. Where did she live? *(With her children, traveling from house to house.)*

11. How did Susanna stay close to her grown children when she was away from them? *(She wrote them letters.)*

12. What special job did Susanna's sons John and Charles have? *(They were preachers.)*

13. When Susanna went to John's church, she heard something that made her realize that trying to be a good person was not the way for her sins to be forgiven. What was the way that she was saved? *(Trusting in what Jesus had done for her when He died on the cross.)*

14. What did Susanna ask her children to do after she died? *(Sing a song of praise to God, just as they had done together when they were young.)*

15. **Discussion Question**: Susanna Wesley depended on God through many troubles, and God used her example to help her sons Charles and John become men who told many people about Jesus. Do you think that doing a job that nobody sees is still important? Tell about someone who has made a difference in your life who may not have received a lot of praise for what he/she did. How do you think God might use the "small" choices you make to one day make a big difference?

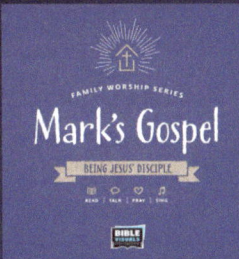

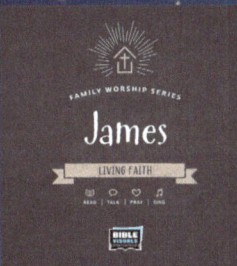
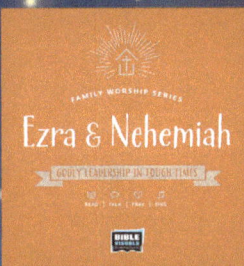

WHAT DOES FAMILY WORSHIP LOOK LIKE IN YOUR HOME?

Many Christian parents recognize the importance of God's Word, but have never seen family worship modeled. BVI's Family Worship Series provides guidance through a simple structure for family worship.

READ – directly from the Bible, skipping nothing
TALK – purposefully, using questions for all ages
PRAY – scripturally, through suggested prayer points
SING – joyfully, following a simple song section

biblevisuals.org/family

HELPING FAMILIES SEE JESUS!
BIBLEVISUALS.ORG

www.ingramcontent.com/pod-product-compliance
Lightning Source LLC
Chambersburg PA
CBHW041540040426
42446CB00002B/169